BIRD'S EYE VIEWS
of Wisconsin Communities

A Preliminary Checklist by ELIZABETH SINGER MAULE

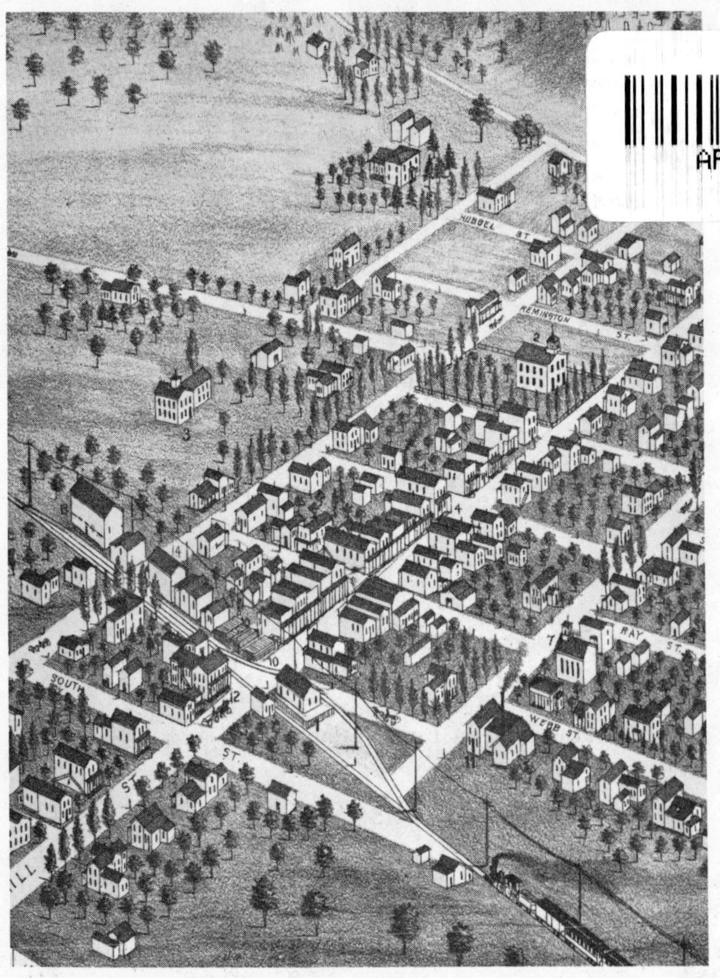

Guides to Historical Resources
THE STATE HISTORICAL SOCIETY OF WISCONSIN
1977

Cover illustration: Bird's eye view of Kenosha,
Wisconsin, 1882. *Preceding page:* Detail from
bird's eye view of Black Earth, Wisconsin.

Library of Congress Cataloging in Publication Data

Maule, Elizabeth Singer.
    Bird's eye views of Wisconsin communities.

    (Guides to historical resources)
    1. Wisconsin--Maps, Pictorial--Bibliography.
2. Lithographs--Wisconsin--Bibliography. I. Title.
II. Series: Wisconsin. State Historical Society.
Guides to historical resources.
Z6027.U5M38   [GA458]   016.769'4'409775   77-24430
ISBN 0-87020-168-9

Bird's eye views of Wisconsin Communities: a preliminary checklist

A bird's eye view is a combination map and mock aerial photograph of

a community. Seemingly, its creators sketched from about 2,000 feet aloft

in a balloon, using what amounts to an isometric perspective and always

drawing streets at an angle to the borders. The results in almost each

case are surprisingly two-dimensional, akin to an engineer's drawing rather

than a fine artist's more three-dimensional work. In the foreground,

closer to the viewer, perspectives appear flatter than in the middle dis-

tance, while in the far distance the horizons seem to rise to the sky.

The foregrounds seem oddly out of place and almost unnecessary. The towns

are always neat, busy, and progressive. Their streets and terrain are

nearly flat, their unimportant buildings similar, their trees all lollipops.

They are peopled with stick-figure citizens who crack whips over teams of

Noah's ark horses. Locomotives belch coloring-book smoke, and ships crowd

together in rivers and harbors, endowing the towns with vitality and bustle.

The towns intentionally appear more active than they were, an attribute

wholly in harmony with the boastful atmosphere of the middle and late

nineteenth century. It is an atmosphere so naive that it merely adds to

the charm of the views and to their popular appeal.

Perspective or panoramic views of cities were by no means novel ideas

in the mid-nineteenth century. The Braun and Hogenberg views, published

in 1572-1618 and listed in the appendix, had the same traits as the later

bird's eyes. But the form enjoyed a great resurgence during the heyday of

the westward movement in the second half of the nineteenth century. As

settlers carved homes and lives out of the wilderness, they wanted to
celebrate their achievements and to point them out pridefully to others.
The bird's eyes served them well.

The expanding lithographic industry also helps account for increased
production of bird's eyes. Lithography had been invented in 1798 by a
Bavarian, who capitalized on the principles that grease and water do not
mix and that each can be applied easily to a single polished stone surface.
Compared to the earlier process of engraving a copper plate, preparing
a stone for printing was cheaper, less time-consuming, and it sacrificed
nothing in detail or quality. The medium was ideal for bird's eye views.

Since Bavaria was the birthplace of lithography, it is perhaps no
accident that by about 1855 Milwaukee, the home of thousands of German
immigrants, was the center of a considerable lithographic industry. Per-
sons such as Henry Seifert, the Guglers, Silas Chapman, Louis Lipman,
Knauber, and Beck & Pauli -- all but Chapman being unmistakably Teutonic --
were active as general printers under their own names or as founders of
companies like the American Oleograph Co., which competed with others in
preparing stones for local artists.

The exact commercial ties between the artists and publishers have not
been studied, and they almost certainly varied. In most cases, however,
artists appear to have acted somewhat independently of the publishers,
who may or may not have suggested the names of likely towns. Usually a
local artist sent his work to one of the Milwaukee or Chicago lithographers.
Sometimes lithographers acted as publishers; other times the lithography
and publishing were handled by different firms. For some time Madison

served as a center for training. Albert Ruger, who was first to achieve
fame as a bird's eye view artist, moved from Michigan to Wisconsin in the
late 1860's and was soon allied with J. J. Stoner, a Madison publisher.
Other important artists such as Thaddeus Fowler and Henry Wellge trained and
worked under Ruger and Stoner before starting their own firms elsewhere.
(Fowler's first view was of Omro, Wisconsin, in 1870, and it was prepared
in Madison.) Ruger and Stoner assuredly trained many less important
artists, too, for suddenly art -- landscape painting, portaits, etchings,
and the crafts -- became successful business enterprises and widespread
avocations nationally. Stoner was so well-known that he acted as publisher
for every bird's eye artist except Lucien Burleigh, who worked out of
Troy, New York. Madison continued to be an important center for the
industry through the 1870's, after which most of the artists had moved to
other areas, perhaps to exploit new markets. By about 1910 the bird's eye
view industry began to decline as the panoramic photograph overtook it.

How were the views actually produced? The artist, who usually took
great pride and pleasure in doing a superlative job, picked an area and
surveyed its communities in one season. He first walked up and down the
streets and sketched every building. Then he would decide on the most
promising aerial vantage point, and he would put his sketches together
accordingly. His manuscript was then transferred to a lithographic stone,
printed, and published. Although no one is sure how many copies of each
were printed, the number was undoubtedly small because the views appealed
only to townspeople. This helps to explain why so few copies of each sur-
vive today. It is highly possible that, as panoramic camera technology

improved, the artists took photographs rather than sketch each building. A
1908 view of Madison, for example, coincides with panoramic photographs
taken that spring.

In their day bird's eye views were commonly used as maps. The important buildings were identified and the streets named with a fair amount of accuracy. They were also, of course, used as colorful decorations and as gifts to friends and relatives. Perhaps more important was their value as promotional advertising for real estate and for companies such as L. S. Sheldon's farm implements enterprise (Madison, 1885). Probably they were used in much the same way gift calendars are.

Art historians have come to appreciate the bird's eye as an example of a native folkart. The urban historian, too, uses them, since the views give a wealth of information about how towns looked and about how they have changed and developed. In conjunction with other maps, the views bring communities alive for everyone who studies them.

In March, 1975, I mailed more than a thousand questionnaires to institutions in the state which seemed likely to have or know about local and area bird's eye views. Approximately fifteen percent of the questionnaires were returned, and from them I have learned about an additional sixty views. Those I have examined or received copies of are included as complete entries in the checklist. I hope eventually to gather what information is missing from the other entries. I am sure that the checklist is by no means complete; there are undoubtedly other views hanging on walls in public and private offices or lying forgotten in attics. If you see a view -- an original, a facsimile, or one that seems to be a variant copy -- please let

me know. I am also interested in learning where there are other copies
of previously identified views. In two or three years the checklist will
be revised and reprinted; I would like it to be as complete as possible
then.

The checklist, limited to those views published as separate items,
has been divided into three sections. The main body includes all currently
known views of Wisconsin cities and towns, where copies of each may be
found, and as much descriptive information as I could gather. The views
are arranged alphabetically, then chronologically, by city name. The
first lines of each entry give all titles quoted directly from the views,
with inconsistencies of spelling and punctuation reproduced. On the next
line are the size of the view (v.) or picture and textual matter, and the
size of the page (p.) on which they were printed. Dimensions are given
in centimeters, height first, then width. In the same line a view is
identified as black and white or tinted. Black and white prints have
a black base plate for linework, lettering, and shading,and usually
one tint base which is gray or green. Those views with two or three tint
bases (tan, blue, and green) are referred to as tinted. Occasionally I
did not know a size or the coloring of the original; such instances have
been marked "n.a." (not available). The next few lines of each entry list
all the names and firms associated with producing each view. Again these
are quoted directly. If there are any insets, each is listed. Finally
all the known locations of each view are given. The State Historical Society
of Wisconsin (SHSW) is always listed first. Views at the Library of Congress
are housed in its Geography and Map Division. Unless otherwise stated,

views are originals. In instances when I know a view exists but have not
seen it myself, I have listed the city name, date, and owner followed by
the phrase "Bibliographical details as yet unavailable." In time I hope
to be able to complete all these entries.

The second part of the checklist is a short addendum. I continually
receive more information, some too late to have been included in the main
body of the text. It is, therefore, in the addendum. Finally, the State
Historical Society's views of cities in other states and countries are
listed in the appendix. Since Madison was one of the early centers of the
bird's eye view industry, it was only natural that views of non-Wisconsin
cities found their way into the Society's Map and Atlas Collection. Another
part of the Collection is sixteenth through eighteenth century European-
produced material documenting the discovery and exploration of North America.
It includes a number of copper engraved and hand-colored late-sixteenth-
century bird's eye views of European cities by George Braun and Franz Hogenberg.
Their perspectives are similar to those used by nineteenth-century artists.
Even community pride as evidenced by what was probably more than normal
hustle and bustle in a port, for example, is evident. On the back, or verso,
of the views is a description in Latin of the city. Sometimes the title of
the view and the title of the text vary. Most include the city's coat of
arms, and occasionally there are pictures of individuals which provide important clues for historians about sixteenth-century Europeans. However,
unlike their later American counterparts, these views depict only major
cities; they were meant to be included in an atlas and not to be issued
separately.

I cannot thank individually all those who took the time to complete
the questionnaire, to answer my inquiries, and to supply me with copies
of views. But I would like especially to thank James L. Nabak, my student
assistant, who kept track of the correspondence and prepared the manuscript
for typing.

Elizabeth Singer Maule

AHNAPEE

[1880. Held by Algoma Schools Administrator. Bibliographical
        details as yet unavailable.]

ALMA

"Alma County Seat of Buffalo County Wisconsin" [1880]

        v. 28 x 67cm.   p. 40 x 71cm.   Black & white
        H. Brosius, del.
        Beck & Pauli, Litho. Milwaukee, Wis.
        Published by Ruger & Stoner, Madison, Wis.
        Inset: Lave's Lumber Mill
        Location: SHSW
                   Prairie Moon Museum, Cochrane

ANTIGO

"A Bird's Eye View of the City of Antigo, Wis. County Seat of
Langlade County. 1886   Population 2500,   June 1882, 250."

        v. 32 x 58cm.   p. 45 x 60cm.   n.a.
        Beck & Pauli Litho. Milwaukee, Wis.
        Copyrighted & Published by Norris, Wellge & Co. No. 205
            Second St. Milwaukee, Wis.
        Insets: First House in Antigo; Weeds Saw Mill; Spring
                 Brook House; North Side of Fifth Ave
        Location: SHSW - copy
                   Library of Congress

[ca. 1907. Held by Duchac Title and Abstract Co., Antigo, Bibliographical
            details as yet unavailable.]

APPLETON

"Appleton Outagamie County, Wisconsin 1867"

        v. 51 x 71cm.   p. 61 x 76cm.   Tinted
        Drawn from Nature by A. Ruger, Chicago
        Chicago Lithographing Co.
        Location: SHSW
                   Library of Congress

(Appleton - cont.)

"Bird's Eye View of Appleton, Wis 1874"

        v. 47 x 82cm.   p. 61 x 91cm.   Tinted
        Drawn & Pub. by Stoner & Vogt
        Am[erican] Oleograph Co. Print.
        Entered According To Act of Congress in the year 1874
            by Stoner & Vogt.
        Location: SHSW - copy
                   Lawrence University

[Appleton 1881?]

        v. n.a.   p. n.a.   Black & white
        Marr Richards Eng. Mil.
        Location: Appleton Post Annual Review, December 21, 1882.

                              ASHLAND

"Ashland, the Metropolis of the New Wisconsin," [n.d.]

        v. 32 x 64cm.   p. 39 x 71cm.   Black & white
        Marr. Richards. Eng. Mil, St.P.
        Location: SHSW

"A Bird s Eye View of the City of Ashland, Wis. County Seat of
Ashland Co. 1886"

        v. 35 x 83cm.   p. 50 x 88cm.   n.a.
        Beck & Pauli, Litho. Milwaukee, Wis.
        Copyrighted & Published by Norris, Wellge & Co. No.
            205 Second St. Milwaukee, Wis.
        Insets: The Apostle "Islands" Chequamagon Bay &
                 Ashland; Distances from Ashland
        Location: SHSW - copy
                   Library of Congress

"Ashland, Lake Superior, Wis. 1890. Population 16,000. Increase
in ten years, 11,000. Published by The Ashland Daily Press."

        v. 49 x 100cm.   p. 64 x 104cm.   Black & white
        Drawn by C. J. Pauli, Milwaukee
        Marr & Richards Engraving Co., Milwaukee.
        Copyrighted by The Ashland Daily Press.
        Inset: Prentice Park and Fishery
        Location: SHSW
                   Library of Congress

BARABOO

"Bird's Eye View of Baraboo Sauk County Wisconsin 1870."

      v. 43 x 51cm.   p. 48 x 58cm.   Tinted
      Merchants Lithographing Co. Chicago
      Published by Ruger & Stoner, Madison Wis.
      Insets: Court House; High School
      Location: SHSW

BARTON

[1878. Held by Dr. Richard Driessel, Titusville, FL. Bibliographical
details as yet unavailable.]

BAYFIELD

"Bird's Eye View of Bayfield, Wisconsin, Summer of 1884."

      v. n.a.   p. n.a.   Black & white
      Insets: Court House; La Pointe
      Location: Bayfield County Press, January 9, 1886.

"Birds Eye View of Bayfield, Wis. County Seat of Bayfield County, 1886."

      v. 32 x 51cm.   p. n.a.   n.a.
      H. Wellge Sk.
      Beck & Pauli, Litho. Milwaukee, Wis.
      Copyrighted & Published by Norris, Wellge & Co. No. 205
        Second St. Milwaukee, Wis.
      Inset: Bayfield and the Apostle Islands
      Location: SHSW - copy
            Library of Congress
            Madeline Island Historical Museum, La Pointe

"Bird's Eye View of Bayfield and the Apostle Islands, Lake Superior"
[1893]

      v. n.a.   p. n.a.   n.a.
      Marr-Richards, Mil. St. Paul
      Location: Bayfield County Press January 21, 1893.
         [some editions only]

BEAVER DAM

"Birds Eye View of the City of Beaver Dam Dodge Co., Wisconsin, 1867"

        v. 53 x 61cm.   p. 58 x 71cm.   n.a.
        [Drawn by A. Ruger]
        [Chicago Lithographing Co. 152 & 154, Clark St., Chicago]
        Location: SHSW - facsimile, ca. 1947
                  Library of Congress

"Beaver Dam Dodge, Co. Wis. 1879."

        v. 46 x 62cm.   p. 56 x 66cm.   Black & white
        Beck & Pauli, Lith. Milwaukee, Wis.
        Location: SHSW - copy
        Dodge County Historical Society, Beaver Dam

BELOIT

"Beloit. Rock County. Wisconsin. 1874."

        v. 48 x 65cm.   p. n.a.   Tinted
        J. Knauber & Co. Print. Milwaukee Wis.
        Pub. by J. J. Stoner, Madison, Wis.
        Insets: Beloit College; Beloit High School;
                 Memorial Hall
        Location: SHSW - hand colored facsimile, 1975?

"Perspective Map of Beloit, Wis. 1890"

        v. 41 x 70cm.   p. 58 x 77cm.   n.a.
        Copyrighted & Published by American Publishing Co.
            Cor. South Water & Ferry Sts. Milwaukee, Wis.
        Insets: Williams Engine Works; Eclipse Wind Engine Co.;
                 John Foster & Co.
        Location: SHSW - copy
                  Library of Congress

BERLIN

"Bird's Eye View of the City of Berlin Green Lake Co. Wisconsin, 1867"

        v. 46 x 62cm.   p. 57 x 73cm.   n.a.
        Drawn by A. Ruger
        Chicago Lithographing Co. 152 & 154, Clark St. Chicago
        Insets: West Side Public School; High School
        Location: SHSW - copy
                  Library of Congress
                  Clark School Museum, Berlin

(Berlin - cont.)

[1892. Held by Berlin Historical Society, Bibliographical details
as yet unavailable.]

BLACK EARTH

"Bird's Eye View of Black Earth. Looking from the North West, 1876"

>   v. 24 x 31cm.   p. 30 x 35cm.   Black & white
>   D. Bremmer & Co. Lith. Milwaukee.
>   Location: SHSW

[ca. 1883. Held by Wilma Mickelson Pine, Black Earth,
Bibliographical details as yet unavailable.]

BLACK RIVER FALLS

"Birds Eye View of Black River Falls, Jackson County, Wis Looking
Southwest." [1872]

>   v. 38 x 53cm.   p. 47 x 60cm.   Tinted
>   Drawn by H. Brosius.
>   Published by J. J. Stoner, Madison, Wis.
>   Location: SHSW
>   Jackson County Historical Society, Black River Falls
>   P. Hull, Black River Falls
>   D. Struble, Neillsville

BOSCOBEL

"Bird's Eye View of Boscobel Grant Co. Wisconsin. 1869"

>   v. 46 x 57cm.   p. 55 x 65cm.   Tinted
>   Chicago Lithographing Co. Clark St.
>   Published by Ruger & Stoner Madison, Wisconsin.
>   Location: SHSW
>   Library of Congress

BRODHEAD

"Brodhead, Wis. 1871."

        v. 34 x 49cm.   p. 42 x 55cm,   Tinted
        Drawn by H. H. Bailey
        Lith. by Doniat & Zastrow, Milwaukee.
        Location: SHSW
                Memorial Library, Brodhead

BURLINGTON

"Burlington, Wis. 1871"

        v. 32 x 50cm.   p. ca. 32 x 50cm.   Tinted
        Drawn by H. H. Bailey
        Chicago Lithographing Co.
        Published by T. M. Fowler & Co. Madison, Wis.
        Location: SHSW - copy
                Burlington Historical Society, Burlington

"Burlington, Wis. 1896"

        v. 31 x 51cm.   p. 34 x 51cm.   Black & white
        Drawn & Published by C. J. Pauli 234 22nd St.
          Milwaukee, Wis.
        Inset: McCanna's Edgew[ater?]
        Location: SHSW - copy
                Burlington Historical Society, Burlington

CEDARBURG

"Cedarburg, Wisconsin" [1882]

        v. 42 x 55cm. p. n.a.   Black & white
        Drawn & Published by H. Wellge & J. Bach. Milwaukee
        Lith. by Beck & Pauli, Milwaukee, Wis.
        Inset: Cedarburg Brewery
        Location: Cedarburg Public Library, Cedarburg

(Cedarburg - cont.)

"Cedarburg, Wis. 1892"

> v. 44 x 63cm.   p. n.a.   Black & white
> Insets: Cedarburg Brewery; Cedarburg Woolen Mills;
>   Cedarburg wire & wire nail factory; Cedarburg
>   Mills; Cedarburg Rattan & Willow-ware Co.;
>   Frank Chicory Co.; Hilgen Manufacturing Co.;
>   Hilgen Spring Park
> Location: Cedarburg Public Library, Cedarburg

CHILTON

"View of Chilton Wis. 1878 Pop. about 2,000"

> v. 44 x 59cm.   p. n.a.   Black & white
> Drawn & Publ. by H. Wellge & J. Bach.
> Insets: P. H. Becker's Brewery and Summer Garden;
>   Chilton House; Gutheil's Block; Residence of
>   Mr. P. Kettenhofen; Residence of Hon. Geo.
>   Baldwin
> Location: Bill Engler, Jr., Chilton

CHIPPEWA FALLS

[1874. Held by Joseph Joas, Chippewa Falls. Bibliographical details
as yet unavailable.]

"Chippewa-Falls, Wis. County-seat of Chippewa-County
1886. Population: 10,000."

> v. 45 x 67cm.   p. 58 x 77cm.   n.a.
> H. W[ellge]
> Beck & Pauli, Litho. Milwaukee, Wis.
> Copyrighted & Published by Norris, Wellge & Co.
>   No. 107 Wells St. Milwaukee, Wis. 1885.
> Location: SHSW - copy
>   Library of Congress

(Chippewa Falls - cont.)

"Chippewa-Falls, Wisconsin, County-Seat of Chippewa County,
1907. Population 12,000."

       v. 45 x 77cm.   p. 54 x 82cm.   n.a.
       H. W[ellge] SK 1906
       Copyrighted 1906 by H. Wellge, Milwaukee, Wis.
       Insets: Chippewa Lumber & Boom Co.; Opera House
              Block; Chippewa Falls Furniture Co.; J.
              Leinenkugel Brewing Co.
       Location: SHSW - copy
              Library of Congress
              J. Joas, Chippewa Falls

CLINTON

"Clinton, Wis. 1871."

       v. n.a.   p. n.a.   n.a.
       Drawn by H. H. Bailey
       Lith. by Doniat & Zastrow, Milwaukee
       Location: SHSW - copy
              Chicago Historical Society

COLUMBUS

"Bird's Eye View of Columbus Columbia Co. Wisconsin 1868"

       v. 43 x 61cm.   p. 56 x 71cm.   n.a.
       Drawn by A. Ruger
       Chicago Lithographing Co. 152 & 154, Clark St.
         Chicago
       Location: SHSW - copy
              Library of Congress

DARLINGTON

"Bird's Eye View of Darlington Lafayette County Wis. 1871
Looking North West"

       v. 37 x 50cm.   p. 45 x 58cm.   Tinted
       Drawn by H. Brosius
       Insets: Public School; County Court House and Jail
       Location: SHSW

(Darlington - cont.)

"View of Darlington, Wis. County Seat of Lafayette Co. 1881."

>   v. 29 x 51cm.   p. 38 x 59cm.   Black & white
>   Beck & Pauli, Lith., Milwaukee, Wis.
>   Pub. by J. J. Stoner, Madison, Wis.
>   Location: SHSW

"Darlington, Wis. 1896"

>   v. 36 x 55cm.   p. 57 x 73cm.   Black & white
>   Drawn and Published by C. J. Pauli, 234 Twenty-second
>   Street, Milwaukee, Wis.
>   Location: SHSW

DELAVAN

"Delavan. Walworth Co. Wisconsin. 1884."

>   v. 37 x 59cm.   p. 51 x 76cm.   n.a.
>   H. Brosius Del.
>   Beck & Pauli, Litho. Milwaukee, Wis.
>   Published by J. J. Stoner, Madison, Wis.
>   Copyrighted 1884 by J. J. Stoner, Madison, Wis.
>   Inset: State Institute for Deaf and Dumb
>   Location: SHSW - copy
>   Library of Congress

DE PERE

"De Pere, Wis. 1871"

>   v. n.a.   p. n.a.   n.a.
>   Drawn by H. H. Bailey
>   Chicago Lithographing Co.
>   Location: SHSW - copy

"De Pere, Wis. 1893. Looking North."

>   v. n.a.   p. n.a.   n.a.
>   Drawn and Published by C. J. Pauli, 726 Central Avenue,
>   Milwaukee, Wis.
>   Insets: W. A. Bingham's Store, General Merchandise, West
>   De Pere; Columian Mills
>   Location: SHSW - copy

DODGEVILLE

"Bird's Eye View of Dodgeville. Iowa County Wis.
Looking South East." [1875]

        v. 40 x 51cm.   p. 47 x 59cm.   Tinted
        Drawn by H. Brosius,
        Insets: High School; County Court House
        Location: SHSW

EAU CLAIRE

"Bird's Eye View of the City of Eau Claire
Eau Claire County Wis. 1872 Looking North East,"

        v. 51 x 65cm.   p. 57 x 73cm.   Tinted
        Drawn by H. Brosius
        Insets: West Side Public School; East Side Public
               School
        Location: SHSW
               Chippewa Valley Museum, Eau Claire

"Eau Claire, Wisconsin. 1880."

        v. 45 x 71cm.   p. 57 x 77cm.   Black & white
        Beck & Pauli, Lith., Milwaukee, Wis.
        Pub. by J. J. Stoner, Madison, Wis,
        Inset: Lower Part of West Side
        Location: SHSW
               Chippewa Valley Museum, Eau Claire

"Eau Claire, Wis. 1891. Looking West,"

        v. 48 x 89cm.   p. 60 x 97cm.   Black & white
        Drawn and Published by C. J. Pauli, 726 Central Ave.
          Milwaukee.
        Location: SHSW - copy
               Eau Claire Public Library
               Chippewa Valley Museum, Eau Claire

ELROY

"Elroy Juneau, Co. Wisconsin, 1879."

        v. 22 x 40cm.   p. 36 x 51cm.   Black & white
        Beck & Pauli Lith. Milwaukee, Wis.
        Pub. by J. J. Stoner, Madison, Wis,
        Location: SHSW

FLORENCE

"Bird's Eye View of Florence, Wis. 1881."

  v. 19 x 42cm. p. 33 x 50cm. Black & white
  J. J. Stoner, Pub. Madison, Wis.
  Location: SHSW

FOND DU LAC

"Fond du Lac Wisconsin 1867."

  v. 52 x 71cm. p. 59 x 75cm. Tinted
  Drawn by A. Ruger
  Chicago Lithographing Co. 152 & 154; Clark St, Chicago.
  Location: SHSW
      Library of Congress
  Published in facsimile form, 1974, by Fond du Lac County
    Historical Society

"Fond du Lac, Wis., 1896. Looking North-West."

  v. 43 x 83cm. p. 58 x 83cm. Black & white
  Drawn and Published by C. J. Pauli, 234 22nd St.
    Milwaukee, Wis.
  Inset: P. H. Stamm; proposed Lakeside Park
  Location: SHSW - copy
      Fond du Lac Public Library
  Published in facsimile form, 1974, by Fond du Lac County Historical
    Society

FORT ATKINSON

"Bird's Eye View of Fort Atkinson Jefferson County
Wisconsin 1870 Looking North East"

  v. 38 x 52cm. p. 48 x 62cm. Tinted
  Merchants Lithographing Co. Chicago
  Published by Ruger & Stoner Madison, Wis.
  Location: SHSW
      Hoard Historical Museum, Fort Atkinson

(Fort Atkinson - cont.)

"Bird's Eye View of the City of Fort Atkinson. Jefferson Co, Wis 1880,"

       v. 27 x 50cm.   p. 40 x 60cm.   Black & white
       Location: SHSW - copy
                Hoard Historical Museum, Fort Atkinson

"Ft. Atkinson, Wis. 1893. Looking Northwest,"

       v. 39 x 52cm.   p. 58 x 75cm.   Black & white
       Drawn and Published by C. J. Pauli, 726 Central Avenue,
          Milwaukee, Wis.
       Location: SHSW - copy
                Hoard Historical Museum, Fort Atkinson

GRAND RAPIDS

"Bird's Eye View of the City of Grand Rapids. Wood Co, Wis, 1874"

       v. 56 x 87cm.   p. 66 x 91cm.   Tinted
       Drawn & Published by A. J. Cleveland
       A. M. Oleograph. Co, Mil,
       Location: SHSW
                South Wood County Historical Museum,
                  Wisconsin Rapids

GREEN BAY

"Green Bay and Fort Howard Brown Co. Wisconsin 1867"

       v. 50 x 71cm.   p. 60 x 76cm,   n,a.
       Drawn by A. Ruger
       Chicago Lithographing Co, 152 & 154 Clark St.
          Chicago
       Location: SHSW - copy
                Library of Congress
                R. Paye, Green Bay

HARTFORD

"Panoramic View of Hartford Washington Co. Wisconsin. 1879"

        v. 28 x 48cm.   p. 36 x 52cm.   Black & white
        Beck & Pauli Lith. Milwaukee, Wis.
        Pub. by J. J. Stoner, Madison, Wis.
        Location: SHSW
                   Hartford Public Library, Hartford

HORICON

"Horicon, Wis. 1892. Looking North-East"

        v. 29 x ca. 48cm.   p. ca. 40 x 50cm.   Black & white
        Drawn and Published by C. J. Pauli, Milwaukee, Wis.
        Location: SHSW - copy
                   Dodge County Historical Society, Beaver Dam

HUDSON

"Bird's Eye View of the City of Hudson St. Croix County Wisconsin [sic]
1870"

        v. 49 x 59cm.   p. 56 x 72cm.   n.a.
        Merchants Lith. Co. Chicago
        Published by Ruger & Stoner, Madison, Wis.
        Insets: Court House; Public School
        Location: SHSW - copy
                   Library of Congress
                   St. Croix Historical Society, Hudson

"Panoramic view of the City of Hudson St. Croix, Co.
Wisconsin, 1879. Looking North West."

        v. 29 x 55cm.   p. 38 x 61cm.   Black & white
        Beck & Pauli Lith. Milwaukee, Wis.
        Pub. by J. J. Stoner, Madison, Wis.
        Location: SHSW - copy
                   Milwaukee Public Library, Milwaukee

HURLEY

"Hurley, Wis. Ashland County. 1886."

        v. 24 x 47cm.   p. 36 x 56cm.   n.a.
        Beck & Pauli, Litho. Milwaukee, Wis.

(Hurley - cont.)

       Copyrighted & Published by Norris, Wellge & Co. No. 205
          Second St. Milwaukee, Wis.
       Insets: Mining at the Colby; Hurley in 1885;
          North Front of Silver St.
       Location: SHSW - copy
          Library of Congress

HUSTISFORD

"Hustisford, Wis. Dodge County. 1885."

       v. 23 x 46cm.   p. 40 x ca. 50cm.   Black & white
       Beck & Pauli, Litho. Milwaukee
       Pub. by Norris, Wellge & Co. 107 Wells St. Milwaukee,
          Wis. 1885.
       Location: SHSW - copy
          Village Hall, Hustisford

JANESVILLE

"Janesville, Wis. Looking Down the River, in 1877."

       v. 44 x 62cm.   p. 56 x 70cm.   Tinted
       Lith & Printed, by C. H. Vogt & Co. Milwaukee, Wis.
       Location: SHSW

JEFFERSON

"Bird's Eye View of Jefferson Jefferson County Wisconsin 1870.
Looking North East."

       v. 48 x 58cm.   p. 55 x 66cm.   Tinted
       Chicago Lithographing Co.
       Published by Ruger & Stoner, Madison, Wis.
       Insets: Jefferson Liberal Institute; Court House
       Location: SHSW
          Library of Congress

KAUKAUNA

"Bird's Eye View of the Village of Kaukauna Wisconsin." [1882]

     v. n.a.   p. n.a.   Black & white
     Marr-Richards Eng. Mil, St. Paul
     Location: Appleton Post Annual Review, December 21, 1882.

"Kaukauna, Wis. Outagamie County. 1886"

     v. 45 x 63cm.   p. 56 x 73cm.   Black & white
     H. Wellge, Del.
     Beck & Pauli, Litho. Milwaukee, Wis.
     Published by Norris, Wellge & Co. No. 205 Second St.
        Milwaukee, Wis.
     Copyrighted for The Kaukauna Sun.
     Insets: The Sun Office; North Kaukauna; S. Kaukauna
     Location: SHSW

KENOSHA

"Kenosha, Wis. 1882"

     v. n.a.   p. n.a.   Black & white
     Beck & Pauli Lith. Milwaukee, Wis.
     Location: Appleton Post Annual Review, December 21, 1882.

KEWASKUM

"Panoramic View of Kewaskum Washington Co, Wis. 1878 Looking
to the North East"

     v. 23 x 38cm.   p. 33 x 44cm.   Black & white
     Location: SHSW
        E. Heidner, West Bend

KEWAUNEE

"Bird's Eye View of Kewaunee, County Seat of Kewaunee Co. Wis. 1880"

     v. n.a.   p. 28 x 40cm.   Black & white
     Beck & Pauli, Litho. Milwaukee, Wis.
     Published by J. J. Stoner, Madison, Wis.
     Location: SHSW - copy
        Kewaunee County Jail Museum, Kewaunee

(Kewaunee - cont.)

"Kewaunee, Wis. 1893. Looking West."

>   v. n.a.   p. 64 x 77cm.   Black & white
>   Drawn and Published by C. J. Pauli, 726 Central Avenue,
>   Milwaukee, Wis.
>   Inset: The Kewaunee and Frankfort Car Ferry Line
>   Location: SHSW - copy
>   Kewaunee County Jail Museum, Kewaunee

KILBOURN CITY

"Kilbourn City, Wis. 1870."

>   v. 27 x 39cm.   p. 38 x 48cm.   Tinted
>   Drawn by H. H. Bailey
>   Lith. by Doniat & Zastrow, Milwaukee.
>   Location: SHSW

LA CROSSE

"Bird's Eye View of the City of La Crosse Wisconsin 1867."

>   v. 53 x 72cm.   p. 60 x 75cm.   Tinted
>   Drawn by A. Ruger
>   Chicago Lithographing Co. 152 & 154 Clark St.
>   Chicago.
>   Insets: 3rd Ward School; Res. of C. Seymour; Res. of
>   H. Moeller; Res. of G. C. Hixon; Court House &
>   Jail; H. T. Rumsey; Res. of Maj. Gen. G. O. Washburn;
>   Res. of L. Lottridge; 1st Ward School
>   Location: SHSW

"La Crosse, Wis. 1873"

>   v. 36 x 60cm.   p. n.a.   n.a.
>   Geo. H. Ellsbury, Del.
>   Entered according to the act of Congress in the
>   year 1873, by Geo. H. Ellsbury.
>   Milwaukee, Lith & Eng Co.
>   Location: SHSW - copy
>   Library of Congress

(La Crosse - cont.)

"La Crosse, Wis." 1876

        v. 44 x 61cm.   p. 55 x 66cm.   Tinted
        Drawn by C. J. Pauli, Milwaukee, Wis. 1876.
        American Oleograph Co. Lith. Milwaukee.
        Location: SHSW
                 La Crosse Historical Society, La Crosse

"La Crosse, Wis. County Seat La Crosse, County. 1887."

        v. 49 x 99cm.   p. 58 x 104cm.   Black & white
        The Beck & Pauli Lith. Co. Milwaukee
        Copyrighted & Published by H. Wellge 205 Second St.
          Milwaukee, Wis.
        Insets: The John Gund Brewing Company; Burlington House;
               Residence of Dr. D. Frank Powell; Residence of
               Mr. N. Birnbaum; [store front window]; C. & J.
               Michel Brewing Co.
        Location: SHSW
                 Library of Congress

LAKE GENEVA

"Geneva, Wis. 1871"

        v. 27 x 44cm.   p. 37 x 54cm.   Tinted
        Drawn by H. H. Bailey
        Chicago Lithographing Co.
        Location: SHSW
                 Public Library, Lake Geneva
                 Mrs. V. Hackett, Lake Geneva

"Bird's Eye View of Lake Geneva Walworth Co, Wis. 1882.
Looking Southwest."

        v. 42 x 77cm.   p. 55 x 86cm.   Black & white
        Drawn by Wellge & Poole
        Beck & Pauli Lithographers, Milwaukee, Wis.
        Published by J. J. Stoner, Madison, Wis.
        Copyright 1882 by J. J. Stoner, Madison, Wis.
        Insets: Lake Geneva Seminary; Lakeside Park; Bon Ami Camp;
               Englewood Camp; The Lucius Newberry [steamship];
               Pishcotaqua Park House; Kay's Park Hotel; The
               Lady of the Lake [steamship]; The Commodore
               [steamship]; Warwick Park
        Location: SHSW

LAKE MILLS

[date unknown. Held by Mr. Metzger, Lake Mills. Bibliographical
details as yet unavailable.]

LANCASTER

"Bird's Eye View of Lancaster Grant County Wis. Looking
North West." [1875]

>   v. 37 x 46cm.   p. 43 x 51cm.   Tinted
>   Drawn by H. Brosius.
>   Published by J. J. Stoner Madison, Wis.
>   Inset: Monument for the Soldiers of Grant County
>   Location: SHSW

LODI

"Lodi, Columbia County, Wisconsin. 1874"

>   v. n.a.   p. n.a.   n.a.
>   J. Knauber & Co. Print.
>   Pub. by J. J. Stoner
>   Inset: Public School
>   Location: Mrs. J. Trindle, Poynette
>   Published in facsimile form by [Reinhold, Karen] Historical
>   Album, n.p., 1973.

LONE ROCK

"Bird's Eye View of Lone Rock Richland Co. Wisconsin. 1879"

>   v. 17 x 26cm.   p. 27 x 34cm.   Black & white
>   Location: SHSW
>   Brewer Library, Richland Center

MADISON

"Birdseye View of Madison, Wis. and its Surroundings." [n.d.]

>   v. 7 x 12cm.   p. 8 x 12cm.   Tinted
>   Location: SHSW

(Madison,- cont.)

"Madison Wisconsin, 1867."

        v. 54 x 72cm.   p. 56 x 74cm.   Tinted
        Drawn by A. Ruger
        Chicago Lith. Co. Chicago
        Insets: University; Rasdall House; Vilas House; Capitol
        Location: SHSW
                   Library of Congress

"Madison. State Capital of Wisconsin. County Seat of Dane
County. 1885."

        v. 47 x 79cm.   p. 59 x 89cm.   Black & white
        H. Wellge, Del.
        Beck & Pauli, Litho. Milwaukee, Wis.
        Copyrighted & Published by Norris, Wellge & Co. No. 107
           Wells St. Milwaukee, Wis. 1885.
        Inset: [State Capitol]
        Location: SHSW - copy
                   Library of Congress

"Madison. State Capital of Wisconsin. County Seat of Dane County.
1885." [Same as above view with advertising for S. L. Sheldon around
view.]

        v. 62 x 79cm.   p. 72 x 106cm.   Black & white
        H. Wellge, Del
        Copyrighted & Published by Norris, Wellge & Co.
           No. 107 Wells St. Milwaukee, Wis, 1885.
        Insets: [State Capitol]; Haworth Check Rower;
                 [Stubble Plow]; [Spring Wagon]; [Two-Seated Buggy];
                 Buffalo Pitts Coal or Wood Burning Traction Engine;
                 [Cutter]; Wm. Ansonwood Open Gear Mower; [One-Horse
                 Hay Rake]; [Cultivator]; Buffalo Pitts Vibrator; Meadow
                 King Mower; "Buckeye" Force Feed Broad-Cast Seeder;
                 The Casaday Sulky Plow; Esterly's Twine Binding Harvester;
                 "Acme" Pulverizing Harrow; Disc Pulverizing Harrow;
                 Gregg Reaper; J. I. Case, "Agitator"; S. L. Sheldon's
                 Offices and Warehouses
        Location: SHSW
                   Library of Congress

"Panoramic View of Madison, Wis.   State Capital of Wisconsin,
University of Wisconsin." 1908

        v. 32 x 61cm.   p. 46 x 71cm.   Tinted
        1908. H. Wellge. SK
        Copyright 1908 by H. Wellge, Milwaukee, Wis.
           Publisher.
        Location: SHSW

(Madison - cont.)

"University of Wisconsin Campus" 1948

        v. 40 x 59cm.   p. 44 x 63cm.   Tinted
        Jerred '48
        Copyright, 1948, by the University of Wisconsin
            Independent Men's Association.
        Location: SHSW

"A Pictorial Map of the University of Wisconsin" 1972

        v. 38 x 84cm.   p. 53 x 97cm.   Black & white
        Copyright, 1972 Glyn Hewson
        Inset: Bascom Hall
        Location: SHSW

MANITOWOC

[1870. J. Knauber, Milwaukee. Held by Loretta Madson, Manitowoc.
Bibliographical details as yet unavailable.]

"Manitiwoc, Wis. 1883"

        v. 25 x 51cm.   p. n.a.   n.a.
        Beck & Pauli Lithographers, Milwaukee, Wis.
        Published by J. J. Stoner, Madison, Wis.
        Location: SHSW - copy

"Manitowoc, Wis." [1895]

        v. 32 x 51cm.   p. n.a.   n.a.
        Drawn and Published by C. J. Pauli, 234 22nd Street,
            Milwaukee, Wis.
        Location: SHSW - copy

MARINETTE

"Bird's Eye View of Marinette, Wis. 1881."

        v. 35 x 84cm.   p. 44 x 89cm.   Black & white
        Beck & Pauli, Lith., Milwaukee, Wis
        Pub. by J. J. Stoner, Madison, Wis.
        Inset: Robt. Merryman Saw Mill, McCartney Saw Mill, Carney-
                Whitbeck & Co. Saw Mill
        Location: SHSW
                    Marinette County Historical Museum, Marinette

MARSHALL

"Marshall Dane Co. Wis. 1879"

        v. 18 x 30cm.   p. 28 x 33cm.   Black & white
        Beck & Pauli, Lith. Milwaukee, Wis.
        Pub. by J. J. Stoner, Madison, Wis.
        Location: SHSW

MARSHFIELD

[1883. J. J. Stoner. Held by Mayor's Office, Marshfield. Bibliographical
details as yet unavailable.]

[1891. C. J. Pauli. Held by Mayor's Office, Marshfield. Bibliographical
details as yet unavailable.]

MAUSTON

"Mauston, Wis. 1870."

        v. 27 x 47cm.   p. 36 x 52cm.   Tinted
        Drawn by H. H. Bailey
        Lith. by Doniat & Zastrow Milwaukee.
        Location: SHSW
                Boorman House, Mauston
                M. Berlein, Mauston

MAYVILLE

"Mayville, Wis. Dodge County. 1885."

        v. 30 x 51cm.   p. 41 x 56cm.   Tinted
        Beck & Pauli, Litho. Milwaukee, Wis.
        Published by Norris, Wellge & Co. No. 107 Wells St.
            Milwaukee, Wis. 1885."
        Location: SHSW - copy
                Mayville Museum, Mayville

MAZOMANIE

"Bird's Eye View of Mazomanie Dane County, Wis." [1875]

        v. 33 x 44cm.   p. 44 x 49cm.   Tinted
        Drawn by H. Brosius.
        C. Shober & Co., Prop. Chicago Lith. Co.
        Published by J. J. Stoner Madison, Wis.
        Location: SHSW

MEDFORD

"Medford, Wis. County Seat of Taylor County Before the
Great Fire May 28th. 1885."

        v. 27 x 46cm.   p. 41 x 56cm.   n.a.
        H. W[ellge]
        Beck & Pauli, Litho,Milwaukee, Wis.
        Copyrighted & Published by Norris, Wellge & Co.
           No. 107 Wells St. Milwaukee, Wis, 1885
        Inset: Medford House
        Location: SHSW - copy
                   Library of Congress

MENASHA

"Menasha, Wis. 1870."

        v. 39 x 50cm.   p. 46 x 55cm.   Tinted
        Drawn by H. H. Bailey
        Lith. by Doniat & Zastrow, Milwaukee
        Inset: National House
        Location: SHSW
                   W. Herziger, Menasha

MENOMINEE RIVER

"Bird's eye view of the towns at the mouth of the Menominee River."
[Menekaune and Marinette, WI and Menominee, MI, ca. 1872,]

        v. 23 x 56cm.   p. 55 x 65cm.   Tinted
        Drawn by O. H. Bailey
        Strobridge & Co. Lith., Cincinnati, O.
        Location: SHSW - copy
                   Marinette County Historical Society

MENOMONEE

"Bird's Eye View of Menomonee Dunn County Wis." [1875]

    v. 36 x 51cm.   p. 45 x 56cm.   Tinted
    Drawn by H. Brosius
    Inset: County Court House
    Location: SHSW

MENOMONEE FALLS

"Menomonee Falls. Waukesha County. Wisconsin 1886"

    v. 22 x 47cm.   p. 39 x 61cm.   n.a.
    Beck & Pauli, Litho. Milwaukee, Wis.
    Copyrighted & Published by Norris, Wellge & Co.
       No. 205 Second St. Milwaukee, Wis.
    Location: SHSW – copy
              Library of Congress

MERRILL

"Bird's Eye View of Merrill, Wis. County Seat Lincoln Co. 1883."

    v. 27 x 78cm.   p. 38 x 87cm.   n.a.
    Drawn by H. Wellge.
    Beck & Pauli, Lithographers, Milwaukee, Wis.
    Copyright secured and published by J. J. Stoner,
       Madison, Wis.
    Location: SHSW – copy
             Library of Congress
             T. B. Scott Free Library, Merrill

MERRILLAN

[1883. Held by Mrs. Harland Anderson, Merrillan. Bibliographical
details as yet unavailable.]

MIDDLETON

"Bird's Eye View of Middleton, Dane County, Wisconsin. 1876."

      v. 23 x 31cm.   p. 30 x 37cm.   Black & white
      Inset: School House
      Location: SHSW
            City Hall, Middleton

MILTON JUNCTION

"Bir'ds Eye View of Milton Junction. Rock Co. Wis. 1881,"

      v. 21 x 38cm,   p. 29 x 44cm.   Black & white
      Location: SHSW

MILWAUKEE

"Panorama of Milwaukee" [n.d.]

      v. 43 x 78cm.   p. n.a.   Tinted
      Chromo Lith. by L. Lipman
      From a Photograph by John P. Hawkins.
      Copyright Secured
      Location: SHSW - copy
            Milwaukee Public Library
            M. Peterman, Elm Grove

"Milwaukee" [n.d.]

      v. n.a.   p. n.a.   n.a.
      Exec. by G. G. Lange [,] Darmstadt [Germany]
      Published by Charles Magnus N.Y.
      Location: SHSW - copy

"View of the City of Milwaukee, Wisconsin." [1852]

      v. 74 x 132cm.   p. 85 x 143cm.   Tinted
      Drawn on Stone & Printed in Oil Colors by Middleton,
         Wallace & Co. Litho. 115 Walnut St. Cincinnati, O.
      Published by J. T. Palmatary
      Location: SHSW

(Milwaukee - cont.)

"Engraving from 84 Year Old Lithograph Shows What Milwaukee Looked
Like in 1853"

        v. 41 x 87cm.   p. 57 x 92cm.   Black & white
        Federal Printing Co., "Preview" No. 3 of Sentinel
           Centennial Edition.
        [Printed in varient form in the Milwaukee Sentinel,
           July 14, 1937.]
        Location: SHSW

"Milwaukee, Wisconsin." 1854

        v. 64 x 103cm.   p. 80 x 122cm.   Tinted
        Geo. J. Robertson, Del.
        D. W. Moody Lith.
        Printed in Chromo by Endicott & Co. N.Y.
        Published by Smith Brothers & Co. 59 Beekman St.
           New York, 1854.
        Location: SHSW

"Milwaukee, Wis." [1873]

        v. 59 x 97cm.   p. 75 x 100cm.   Tinted
        Drawn by H. H. Bailey.
        Milwaukee Lithographing & Engraving Co.
        Published by Holzapfel & Eskuche, Stationers & Booksellers
           443 East Water Street Milwaukee.
        Copyright Secured
        Location: SHSW
                   Library of Congress
                   Milwaukee Public Library, Milwaukee

"Milwaukee, Wis. 1879"

        v. 60 x 98cm.   p. n.a.   n.a.
        Beck & Pauli, Lithographers, Milwaukee, Wis.
        Published by J. J. Stoner & Co., Madison Wis.
        Entered according to act of Congress, in the Year 1879, by
           J. J. Stoner & Co.
        Location: SHSW - copy
                   Library of Congress
                   Milwaukee Public Library, Milwaukee

(Milwaukee - cont.)

"Milwaukee, Wis." 1882

>   v. 32 x 64cm.   p. 45 x 70cm.   n.a.
>   Copyright 1882 by Beck & Pauli, Milwaukee, Wis.
>   Insets: The Menomonee Valley; National Home for
>   Disabled Volunt Soldiers; Looking East from Cor.
>   Ninth & Cedar St; Down the River from North St.
>   Bridge; The Bay from 7th Ward Park; Looking South
>   from Schlitz's Park; The Rolling Mills of Bay View; A
>   Glimpse through a Ravine from Lloyd Street; The Drive
>   on Grand Avenue; CH. M. St. Paul Car and Machine Shops.
>   Location: SHSW - copy
>   Library of Congress

"Map of Electric Railway System. T.M.E.R.&L. Co." 1898

>   v. 49 x 66cm.   p. 55 x 68cm.   Tinted
>   Northwestern Litho. Co. Milwaukee.
>   Copyright 1898 by John I. Beggs. Milwaukee, Wis.
>   Location: SHSW

"Panoramic View of Milwaukee Wis. taken from City Hall Tower" 1898

>   v. 44 x 125cm.   p. n.a.   Tinted
>   Copyright 1898 by the Gugler Lithographic Co. Milwaukee, Wis.
>   Location: SHSW - copy
>   Milwaukee Public Library, Milwaukee

"The Milwaukee Harbor Project" [ca. 1920]

>   v. 24 x 60cm.   p. 30 x 65cm.   Black & white
>   Location: SHSW - copy
>   Milwaukee Public Library, Milwaukee

MINERAL POINT

"Bird's Eye View of Mineral Point Iowa County Wis. 1872 Looking
South East."

>   v. 47 x 57cm.   p. 64 x 73cm.   Tinted
>   Drawn by H. Brosius
>   Location: SHSW

MONDOVI

"Birds-Eye View of the Village of Mondovi." [1877]

       v. 18 x 33cm.   p. 22 x 33cm.   n.a.
       Location: SHSW - copy
              Mondovi Public Library, Mondovi

MONROE

"Monroe, Wis. 1871."

       v. 46 x 62cm.   p. 55 x 67cm.   Tinted
       Drawn by H. H. Bailey.
       Lith by Doniat & Zastrow, Milwaukee.
       Location: SHSW

MUSCODA

"Muscoda Grant Co. Wis. 1879."

       v. 19 x 31cm.   p. 28 x 37cm.   Black & white
       Location: SHSW
              Village Hall, Muscoda

NEENAH

"Neenah, Wis. 1870."

       v. 38 x 58cm.   p. 46 x 65cm.   Tinted
       Drawn by H. H. Bailey
       Lith by Doniat & Zastrow, Milwaukee Wis.
       Location: SHSW
             Doty Park, Neenah
             R. Mueller, Neenah

[1879. Held by Neenah Public Library. Bibliographical details
as yet unavailable.]

NEILLSVILLE

"Bird's Eye View of Neillsville Clark Co. Wisconsin 1880."

    v. 22 x 53cm. p. 32 x 58cm. Black & white
    Beck & Pauli, Lith., Milwaukee, Wis.
    Pub. by J. J. Stoner, Madison, Wis.
    Inset: [Corner Main St. and Road to Fairground]
    Location: SHSW
        D. Struble, Neillsville

NEW LONDON

"New-London, Wis. 1871."

    v. 30 x 48cm. p. 35 x 55cm. Tinted
    Drawn by H. H. Bailey.
    Chicago Lithographing Co.
    Location: SHSW

OCONOMOWOC

"Oconomowoc, Wis. 1870."

    v. 34 x 51cm. p. 43 x 56cm. Tinted
    Drawn by H. H. Bailey.
    Lith. by Doniat & Zastrow, Milwaukee.
    Published by T.M. Fowler & Co. Address - Box 668.
      Madison, Wis.
    Location: SHSW

"View of the City of Oconomowoc, Wis. Waukesha County. 1885."

    v. 41 x 77cm. p. 59 x 83cm. n.a.
    Beck & Pauli, Litho. Milwaukee, Wis.
    Copyrighted & Published by Norris, Wellge & Co.
      No. 107 Wells St. Milwaukee, Wis, 1885.
    Location: SHSW - copy
        Library of Congress
        Waukesha County Museum, Waukesha

OCONTO

"Bird's Eye View of Oconto, Wis. 1871,"

>v. 38 x 50cm.   p. 45 x 55cm.   Tinted
>Drawn & Pub. by T. M. Fowler & H. H. Bailey.
>C H Vogt, Lith.
>Print. Milwaukee Lith & Eng. Co.
>Location: SHSW - copy
>   Oconto County Historical Society, Oconto

OMRO

"Omro, Wis. 1870"

>v. 32 x 50cm.   p. 41 x 55cm.   Tinted
>Chicago Lithographing Co.
>Published by Th. M. Fowler & Co. Address box 668 Madison, Wis.
>Location: SHSW

OSHKOSH

"Oshkosh. Winebago [sic] Co. Wisconsin 1867,"

>v. 52 x 72cm.   p. 58 x 76cm.   n.a.
>Drawn from Nature by A. Ruger
>Chicago Lithographing Co. Chicago
>Location: SHSW - copy
>   Library of Congress
>   Oshkosh Public Museum

"Oshkosh Wis." 1911

>v. n.a.   p. n.a.   n.a.
>.Copyrighted.1911.by.Castle.Pierce.Ptg.Co.
>Location: SHSW - copy

PESHTIGO

"Bird's Eye View of Peshtigo Wisconsin Sept 1871,"

>v. 31 x 41cm.   p. 38 x 46cm.   Tinted
>Chars. Shober & Co. Proprs. Chicago Lith Co.
>Published by T. M. Fowler & Co. Madison, Wis.

(Peshtigo - cont.)

        Location: SHSW
                   Marinette County Historical Museum, Marinette
                   Oconto County Historical Society, Oconto
                   D. Ebert, Green Bay

"Bird's Eye View of Peshtigo, Wis. 1881."

        v. 26 x 47cm.   p. 35 x 52cm.   Black & white
        Beck & Pauli, Lith,, Milwaukee, Wis.
        Pub. by J. J. Stoner, Madison, Wis,
        Location: SHSW
                   Marinette County Historical Museum, Marinette

PLATTEVILLE

"Bird's Eye View of Platteville Grant County Wis. Looking North
East." [1875]

        v. 38 x 51cm.   p. 46 x 56cm,   Tinted
        Drawn by H. Brosius,
        Location: SHSW

PLYMOUTH

"Plymouth, Wis. Sheboygan County, 1870,"

        v. 25 x 42cm.   p. 35 x 47cm.   Tinted
        Drawn by H. H. Bailey,
        Lith. by Doniat & Zastrow, Milwaukee
        Location: SHSW

"Plymouth Sheboygan Co Wis 1879."

        v. n,a.   p.,n.a.   n.a,
        Pub. & Lith. by Beck & Pauli, Milwaukee
        Location: reproduced from original in the Plymouth Review,
                   July 6, 1972.

PORTAGE

"Bird's Eye View of the City of Portage Columbia Co. Wisconsin 1868,"

      v. 48 x 71cm.   p. 58 x 76cm.   n.a.
      Drawn by A. Ruger
      Chicago Lithographing Co. 152 & 154, Clark St. Chicago
      Insets: Public School; Court House
      Location: SHSW - copy
            Library of Congress

POYNETTE

[1882. Held by Poynette Public Library. Bibliographical
details as yet unavailable.]

PRAIRIE DU CHIEN

"Prairie Du Chien Crawford County Wisconsin 1870."

      v. 44 x 59cm.   p. 55 x 71cm.   Tinted
      Chicago Lithog. Co. No. 150 & 154 S. Clark St. Chicago
      Published by Ruger & Stoner, Madison, Wis.
      Location: SHSW
            Library of Congress

PRAIRIE DU SAC

"Bird's Eye View of Prairie Du Sac Sauk County, Wisconsin 1870.
Looking South West."

      v. 33 x 43cm.   p. 42 x 48cm.   Tinted
      Chicago Lithographing Co.
      Pub. by Ruger & Stoner Madison, Wis.
      Location: SHSW
            Library of Congress

PRINCETON

"Princeton, Wis. 1892. Looking North."

    v. 29 x 50cm.   p. 46 x 61cm.   Black & white
    Designed by C. J. Pauli, Milwaukee.
    Inset: Residence of F. T. Yahr.
    Location: SHSW

RACINE

"Bird's Eye View of Racine. Wisconsin. 1874."

    v. 44 x 71cm.   p. 53 x 79cm.   Black & white
    Drawn by H. Brosius
    Chas. Shober & Co. Prop. Chicago Lith. Co.
    Published by J. J. Stoner, Madison, Wis.
    Inset: Racine College
    Location: SHSW

"Racine. Wis. County Seat of Racine Co. 1883 Looking South West."

    v. n.a.   p. n.a.   n.a.
    H. Brosius
    Copyright Secured and Published by J. J. Stoner, Madison, Wis.
    Insets: Horlick's Food Co; J. Miller & Co; Hurlbut.
            Manufacturing Co; Racine College; Johnson & Field;
            M. M Secor; S. Freeman & Sons; Fixen & Hansing;
            The Elkins Jewerly Store; Racine Wagon & Carriage Co;
            Racine Hardware Mfg. Co; Adocate Building; Lathrop
            Bulding [sic]; South End of the City; View of Racine
            taken 1841 from the Corner of 7th and Main Streets.
    Location: SHSW
            Library of Congress

REEDSBURG

"Bird's Eye View of Reedsburg, Sauk County, Wis. 1874."

    v. 31 x 41cm.   p. n.a.   n.a.
    J. Knauber & Co. Print. Milwaukee, Wis.
    Pub. by J. J. Stoner, Madison, Wis.
    Location: SHSW - copy
            Library of Congress
            L. Reed, Reedsburg

RICHLAND CENTER

"Bird's Eye View of Richland Center. Richland County Wis." [1875]

      v. 33 x 53cm.   p. 44 x 57cm.   Tinted
      Drawn by H. Brosius.
      Published by J. J. Stoner, Madison, Wis.
      Location: SHSW
              Brewer Library, Richland Center

RIPON

"Bird's Eye View of the City of Ripon Fond Du Lac Co. Wisconsin, 1867."

      v. 40 x 61cm.   p. 56 x 70cm.   n.a.
      Drawn by A. Ruger
      Chicago Lithographing Co. 152 & 154, Clark St. Chicago.
      Insets: Res. of Hon. A. M. Skefls; Res. of W. Starr, Esq;
             Res. of R. Catlin, Esq; Res. of Dr. F. M. Hubbard;
             Ripon College
      Location: SHSW - copy
              Library of Congress
              Ripon Historical Society, Ripon

[1892. C. J. Pauli. Held by Ripon Historical Society. Bibliographical details as yet unavailable.]

RIVER FALLS

[1880. Held by Area Research Center, University of Wisconsin--River Falls. Bibliographical details as yet unavailable.]

SAUK CITY

"Bird's Eye View of Sauk City. Sauk County, Wisconsin 1870, Looking North East."

      v. 31 x 46cm.   p. 44 x 52cm.   Tinted
      Chicago Lithographing Co.
      Pub. by Ruger & Stoner, Madison, Wis.
      Location: SHSW
              Library of Congress

(Sauk City - cont.)

"Bird's Eye View of Sauk City, Wis. 1883."

      v. 24 x 47cm.   p. 35 x 54cm.   Black & white
      Beck & Pauli, Lithographers, Milwaukee, Wis.
      Published by J. J. Stoner, Madison, Wis.
      Location: SHSW

SHAWANO

[1881. Held by Shawano County Historical Society. Bibliographical
details as yet unavailable.]

SHEBOYGAN

"Sheboygan, Wis. County Seat of Sheboygan Cty. 1885."

      v. 49 x 78cm.   p. 55 x 79cm.   Black & white
      H. Wellge
      Copyrighted & Published by Norris, Wellge & Co. No. 107
         Wells St. Milwaukee, Wis, 1885.
      M. R. Zaegel & Co. Sole Agents for Sale of this Picture.
      Inset: The Jocob J. Vollrath Mfg. Co.
      Location: SHSW
             Library of Congress

SHEBOYGAN FALLS

"Sheboygan Falls, Wis. 1871."

      v. 28 x 38cm.   p. 35 x 43cm.   Tinted
      Drawn by H. H. Bailey.
      The Calvert Lith. Co. Detroit Mich.
      Published by Th. M. Fowler & Co. Address Box 668 Madison, Wis.
      Location: SHSW

STEVENS POINT

[1874. A. J. Cleveland. Held by City Hall, Stevens Point.
Bibliographical details as yet unavailable.]

(Stevens Point - cont.)

"Stevens Point, Wis. 1891. Looking East."

        v. n.a. x 89cm.   p. n.a. x 97cm.   Black & white
        Drawn and Published by C. J. Pauli, 726 Central Ave.,
            Milwaukee, Wis.
        Inset: Water Works
        Location: SHSW

STOUGHTON

"Stoughton, Wis. 1871"

        v. 27 x 41cm.   p. 33 x 47cm.   Tinted
        Drawn by H. H. Bailey
        Chicago Lithographing Co.
        Location: SHSW

"Bird's Eye View of Stoughton, Wis. 1883."

        v. 24 x 54cm.   p. 33 x 58cm.   Black & white
        Beck & Pauli Lithographers, Milwaukee, Wis.
        Published by J. J. Stoner, Madison, Wis.
        Location: SHSW

SUN PRAIRIE

"Birds Eye View of Sun Prairie Dane County Wisconsin" [1875]

        v. 26 x 33cm.   p. 31 x 38cm.   Tinted
        Drawn by H. Brosius
        Published by J. J. Stoner Madison Wis.
        Location: SHSW

SUPERIOR

"Bird's Eye View of Superior, Wis. County Seat of Douglas
County. 1883."

        v. 27 x 80cm.   p. n.a.   n.a.
        H. Wellge Del.
        Beck & Pauli, Lithographers, Milwaukee, Wis.
        Copyright & Published by J. J. Stoner, Madison, Wis.

(Superior - cont.)

                Insets: [Corner 1st. & L Street]; Hotel Roy; Conner's
                           Point; District School; Presbyterian; Roman
                           Catholic; Episcopal; West Side of West Second
                           Street; East Side of West Second Street; Kuy-
                           kendall House; County Court House
                Location: SHSW - copy
                           Library of Congress

"Bird's Eye View of Superior 1893"

                v. 20 x 27cm.   p. 22 x 28cm.   Tinted
                Drawn & Published by Charles Largo.
                Copyright Applied for
                Location: SHSW

"Bird's Eye View Superior, Wisconsin, "The New Steel Center" 1913

                v. 48 x 69cm.   p. 64 x 84cm.   Brown & white
                Bureau of Engraving Mpls.
                Copyright by Bradley-Brink Co. 1913
                Location: SHSW
                           Library of Congress

"The Twin Ports" [Superior, WI & Duluth, MN] 1915

                v. 36 x 90cm.   p. 46 x 95cm.   n.a.
                H. Wellge, Del.
                Rev. 1915 - Russell
                Freeman Eng. Co. Mpls.
                Copyright 1915 by Northern Scenic Publishing Company
                Location: SHSW - copy
                           Library of Congress
                           Evening Telegram Office, Superior

                                  TOMAH

"Tomah, Wis. 1870."

                v. 26 x 41cm.   p. 35 x 45cm.   Tinted
                Drawn by H. H. Bailey
                Lith. by Doniat & Zastrow, Milwaukee.
                Location: SHSW

TWO RIVERS

[1879. Held by SHSW. Bibliographical details as yet unavailable.]

VIROQUA

"Bird's Eye View of Viroqua, C. S. of Vernon Co. Wis. 1879"

      v. 21 x 34cm.   p. 28 x 39cm.   Black & white
      Beck & Pauli Lith. Milwaukee, Wis.
      Pub. by J. J. Stoner, Madison, Wis.
      Location: SHSW

WASHBURN

"Birds-Eye View City of Washburn, Wisconsin." [n.d.]

      v. 28 x 56cm.   p. 43 x 61cm.   n.a.
      by Gene Ford, Artist.
      Location: SHSW - copy

"Birds Eye View of Washburn, Wis. Bayfield, County. 1886"

      v. 33 x 51cm.   p. 46 x 61cm.   n.a.
      Beck & Pauli, Litho., Milwaukee, Wis.
      Copyrighted & Published by Norris, Wellge & Co. No. 205
         Second St. Milwaukee, Wis.
      Inset: Washburn Chequamagon and the Apostle Islands
      Location: SHSW - copy
            Library of Congress

"Washburn, Wis. 1896"

      v. 37 x 55cm.   p. 43 x 60cm.   n.a.
      Drawn, Published and Copyrighted by L. H. Ruggles.
      Insets: Opera Block; Norwegian Lutheran Church; Washburn Meat
           Market; Walker High School; W. H. Lemke's Store; St.
           John's Episcopal Church; Hotel Washburn; Scandinavian
           Congregational Church; Lincoln School; Norwegian Lutheran
           Trinity Church; Bank of Washburn Building; Congregational
           Church; M. E. Church; Court House; Owen & Frost, Druggists;
           Swedish Lutheran Church; Bayfield County Bank; Roman
           Catholic Church; Town Hall; German Evangelical church.
      Location: SHSW - copy

WATERLOO

"Bird's eye view of Waterloo Jefferson County Wisconsin."
[1875]

        v. 34 x 52cm.   p. 47 x 58cm.   Tinted
        Drawn by H. Brosius
        Published by J. J. Stoner Madison Wis.
        Location: SHSW
                Jack Hyer, Waterloo

WATERTOWN

"Watertown Jefferson Co. Wisconsin. 1867."

        v. 52 x 72cm.   p. 59 x 76cm.   n.a.
        Drawn from Nature by A. Ruger
        Chicago Lithographing Co. 152 & 154 Clark St. Chicago
        Location: SHSW - copy
                Library of Congress
                Octagon House, Watertown

"The City of Watertown, Wis. Dodge & Jefferson Counties 1885."

        v. 50 x 80cm.   p. 58 x 87cm.   n.a.
        Beck & Pauli, Litho. Milwaukee, Wis.
        Copyrighted & Published by Norris, Wellge & Co.
          No. 107 Wells St. Milwaukee, Wis, 1885.
        Inset: [Picture of a house]
        Location: SHSW - copy
                Library of Congress
                Octagon House, Watertown

WAUKESHA

"Bird's Eye View of Waukesha Waukesha County Wisconsin 1874. Looking
South West"

        v. 50 x 61cm.   p. 55 x 67cm.   Black & white
        Pub. by J. J. Stoner Madison, Wis.
        Insets: State Industrial School; Court House; Fountain
                Spring, House.
        Location: SHSW
                Waukesha Public Library, Waukesha
                Waukesha County Museum, Waukesha

(Waukesha, cont.)

"Waukesha, Wis. 1880"

        v. 43 x 55cm.   p. ca. 55 x ca. 68cm.   Black & white
        J. Knauber & Co. Lith. Milwaukee.
        Inset: Analysis of Silurian Springs.
        Location: SHSW - copy
                Waukesha County Museum, Waukesha

"Bird's Eye View of Waukesha, C. S. of Waukesha Co. Wis. 1880"

        v. 39 x 65cm.   p. 51 x 70cm.   Black & white
        H. Wellge Sk.
        Beck & Pauli Lith. Milwaukee, Wis.
        Pub. by J. J. Stoner, Madison, Wis.
        Entered according to act of Congress in the year 1879,
           by J. J. Stoner.
        Location: SHSW
                Library of Congress
                Waukesha County Museum, Waukesha

"Waukesha, Wis. County Seat of Waukesha County. 1887."

        v. 38 x 66cm.   p. ca. 55 x ca. 75cm.   Black & white
        Drawn by H. Wellge
        The Beck & Pauli Lith. Co. Milwaukee
        Copyrighted & Published by Henry Wellge & Co. Cor. Wells
           & Second St. Milwaukee, Wis.
        Insets: Spring City Hotel; The Arcadian Mineral Spring
                Company; The Hadfield Cos. Quarries & Works;
                Hyde Park Hotel
        Location: SHSW - copy
                Waukesha County Museum, Waukesha

"The Lake Region of Waukesha County, Wisconsin. Looking North
from Government Hill." [ca. 1911]

        v. 28 x 70cm.   p. 38 x 74cm.   Tinted
        Published and Copyrighted by the Marr & Richards Eng.
           Co., Milwaukee, Wis.
        Facsimile Waukesha County Historical Society, Inc., c1975.
        Location: SHSW

WAUPACA

"Waupaca, Wis. 1871."

       v. 31 x 44cm.   p. 37 x 49cm.   Tinted
       Drawn by H. H. Bailey
       Chicago Lithographing Co.
       Published by Th. M. Fowler & Co. Address Box:668,
         Madison, Wis.
       Location: SHSW

WAUPUN

"Waupun Wis. 1870."

       v. 26 x 41cm.   p. 32 x 45cm.   Tinted
       Drawn by H. H. Bailey.
       Chicago Lithographing Co.
       Location: SHSW

"View of the City of Waupun, Wis. Situated in Fond du Lac
& Dodge Counties. 1885,"

       v. 40 x 62cm.   p. 47 x 62cm.   Black & white
       H. Wellge.
       Beck & Pauli, Litho. Milwaukee, Wis.
       Copyrighted & Published by Norris, Wellge & Co. No. 107
         Wells St. Milwaukee, Wis, 1885.
       Insets: South Side of Main-Street; Althouse, Wheeler
           & Co. Windmills and Pumps.
       Location: SHSW
           J. Laird, Waupun

WAUSAU

"Bird's Eye View of the City of Wausau, Wis. County Seat of Marathon
Co. 1879."
       v. 31 x 51cm.   p. 41 x 61cm.   n.a.
       Facsimile Employers Insurance of Wausau, 1976?
       Location: SHSW
           Employers Insurance of Wausau, Wausau

"Wausau, Wis. 1891. Looking North."

       v. 51 x 90cm.   p. 60 x 95cm.   Black & white
       Drawn and Published by C. J. Pauli, 726 Central Ave.,
         Milwaukee, Wis.
       Location: SHSW
           Marathon County Historical Society, Wausau

WAUWATOSA

"Looking East from Wauwatosa. Wauwatosa and the Western Suburbs
of Milwaukee. Mean Elevation Above Lake Michigan 180 Feet. 1892."

     v. 42 x 74cm.   p. 55 x 82cm.   n.a.
     Copyrighted & Published by the Marr & Richards
        Engraving Co.
     Inset: [Advertisement for] Warner Bros. & Wambold
     Location: SHSW - copy
           Library of Congress
           Milwaukee Public Library, Milwaukee

WEST BEND

"West Bend. Washington Co. Wis. 1878. Looking to the North West."

     v. 27 x 49cm.   p. 33 x 59cm.   n.a.
     Location: SHSW - copy
           E. Heidner, West Bend

"West Bend, Wis. 1892. Looking West."

     v. 27 x 49cm.   p. 39 x 58cm.   n.a.
     Designed by C. J. Pauli, Milwaukee
     Location: SHSW

WEST SUPERIOR

"Perspective Map of West Superior, Wis." 1887

     v. 38 x 55cm.   p. 48 x 65cm.   n.a.
     Drawn by Henry Wellge & Co. Cor. Wells & Second St.
       Milwaukee Wis.
     Copyrighted 1887 by A. L. Langellier
     Location: SHSW - copy
           Library of Congress

"Bird's-Eye View of West Superior, and Superior, Wis." 1890

     v. 35 x 54cm.   p. 40 x 54cm.   Black & white
     W. Hapin?
     Insets: Wright Farm in 1855; First Building in
           Superior 1859
     Location: Frank Leslie's Illustrated Newspaper,
           July 26, 1890.

WEYAUWEGA

"Weyauwega, Wis. 1870."

>   v. 26 x 33cm.   p. 36 x 39cm.   Tinted
>   Drawn by H. H. Bailey
>   Lith. by Doniat & Zastrow, Milwaukee, [WI]
>   Location: SHSW
>   Little Red Schoolhouse Museum, Weyauwega
>   E. Fenelon, Weyauwega

WHITEWATER

"Bird's Eye View of the City of Whitewater Walworth County
Wisconsin 1870"

>   v. 45 x 60cm.   p. 56 x 68cm.   Tinted
>   Merchants Lith. Co. Chicago.
>   Published by Ruger & Stoner.
>   Location: SHSW

"View of the City of Whitewater, Wis. Walworth-County. 1885."

>   v. 40 x 78cm.   p. 55 x 87cm.   n.a.
>   Beck & Pauli, Litho. Milwaukee, Wis.
>   Copyrighted & Published by Norris, Wellge & Co. No.
>   107 Wells St. Milwaukee, Wis, 1885.
>   Insets: Center-street (North Side);
>   Center-street (South Side);
>   Main-street
>   Location: SHSW - copy
>   Library of Congress
>   Whitewater Public Library, Whitewater
>   Whitewater Historical Society, Whitewater
>   Whitewater City Hall, Whitewater

WISCONSIN DELLS

See Kilbourn City.

WISCONSIN RAPIDS

See Grand Rapids.

APPENDIX

ALEXANDRIA, EGYPT

"Alexandria"

       v. 36 x 48cm   p. 41 x 54cm   Hand-colored
       Text on verso.
       [Braun & Hogenberg, v.2, no. 56]
       Location: SHSW

AMSTERDAM, NETHERLANDS

"Amstelredamum"

       v. 34 x 49cm   p. 41 x 56cm   Hand Colored
       Text on verso
       [Braun & Hogenberg, v. 1, no. 21]
       Inset: [man and woman in contemporary dress]
       Location: SHSW

ANGERS, FRANCE

"An deg auum vulgo Angiers."

       v. 18 x 24cm   p. 42 x 52cm   Hand-colored
       Text on verso.
       Delineauit G. Houfnaglius Anno Dni. 1561
       [Braun & Hogenberg, v. 5, no. 20]

ANTWERP, BELGIUM

"Anverpia"

       v. 34 x 49cm.   p. 41 x 56cm   Hand-colored
       Text on verso
       [Braun & Hogenberg, v. 1, no. 18]

ASHVILLE, NC

"Bird's Eye View of the City of Ashville, North Carolina.
Population 1880, 2610; 1890 11500. 1891."

        v. 56 x 74cm   p. 70 x 81cm   Black & white
        Burleigh Lithographing Establishment, Troy, N.Y.
        Published by Ruger & Stoner, Madison, Wis.
        Insets: Battery Park Hotel; Winyah Sanitarium;
                Extension of South Main Street; Kenilworth Inn
        Location: SHSW
                Library of Congress

BOSTON HARBOR, MA

"Boston Harbor." 1897

        v. 31 x 54cm.   p. 36 x 55cm.   Tinted
        Geo. H. Walker & Co. Lith. Boston
        Copyright 1897 by Geo. H. Walker & Co. Boston
        Location: SHSW

BRISTOL, NH

"Bristol Grafton County N.H. 1884"

        v. 37 x 58cm   p. 46 x 60cm   Black & white
        Beck & Pauli, Litho. Milwaukee, Wis.
        Published by Geo. E. Norris, Brockton, Mass.
        Inset: Extension of Lake St.
        Location: SHSW

BRUSSELS, BELGIUM

"Bruxella"

        v. 33 x 48cm   p. 41 x 56cm   Hand-colored
        Text on verso
        [Braun & Hogenberg, v. 1, no. 15]
        Location: SHSW

CADIZ, SPAIN

"Gades Ab Occiduis Insulae Partibu."

        v. 37 x 49cm   p. 42 x 53cm   Hand-colored
        Text on verso
        Depingebat Georg Houfnagius, Anno 1564
        [Braun & Hogenberg, v. 5, no. 5]
        Insets: Canis leporarius ex indijs
                Occidentilib allatus Ao. 1565;
                Auis sive pica Peruviana allata Anno 1578.
        Location: SHSW

CALARIS

"Calaris"

        v. 9 x 12cm   p. 41 x 55cm   Hand-colored
        Text on verso.
        [Braun & Hogenberg, v. 1, no. 51]
        Location: SHSW

CALIFORNIA

"Bird's Eye View of California. The Morning Call Premium
Map." [n.d.]

        v. 52 x 72cm   p. 56 x 77cm   Tinted
        Schmidt Label & Lith Co. S[an] F[rancisco]
        Location: SHSW

CEDAR RAPIDS, IA

"Cedar Rapids, IA   1889"

        v. 61 x 87cm   p. 69 x 91cm   n.a.
        Drawn & Published by C. J. Pauli & Co, Milwaukee
        Insets: T. M. Sinclair & Co; Partial View of Seed
                Farm of Henry Higley; Shaver & Dow's Cracker
                Factory; West Side Roller Mill Co.; Merritt
                & Allen, Planning Mill; Sutliff Bros.; Williams
                & Hunting; Whiting Manufacturing Co; Greene's
                Opera House; Residence of C. M. Merritt; W. S.
                Roller Mill Co. Henry G. Higley's Green Houses
        Facsimile, 1973, by Gerald A. Noble, Hiawatha, IA
        Location: SHSW - copy

CHICAGO, IL

"The City of Chicago." 1892

        v. 53 x 82cm   p. 56 x 95cm   Tinted
        Copyright 1892, by Currier & Ives. N.Y.
          New York Published by Currier & Ives, 115 Nassau St.
        Location: SHSW
               Library of Congress

COLOGNE, WEST GERMANY

"Colonia Agrippina"

        v. 33 x 78cm   p. 41 x 56cm   Hand-colored
        Text on verso
        [Braun & Hogenberg, v. 1, no. 39]
        Location: SHSW

CHOMUTOV, CZECHOSLOVAKIA

"Commoda vulgo Comethau Bohemiae ciuitas."

        v. 19 x 47cm   p. 21 x 53cm   Hand-colored
        Text on verso
        Communicauit G. Houfnaglius, depic Fum a filio Ao. 1617.
        [Braun & Hogenberg, v. 6, no. 25]
        Location: SHSW

CÓRDOBA, SPAIN

"Corduba."

        v. 34 x 50cm   p. 42 x 53cm   Hand-colored
        Text on verso
        [Braun & Hogenberg, v. 6, no. 5]
        Location: SHSW

ČÁSLAV, CZECHOSLOVAKIA

"Czaslavium vulgo Czasla Bohemiae Civitas."

        v. 19 x 47cm   p. 21 x 53cm   Hand-colored
        Text on verso
        Communicauit G. Houfnaglius, depic Fum a filio Ao. 1617.
        [Braun & Hogenberg, v. 6, n. 25]
        Location: SHSW

EL ESCORIAL, SPAIN

"Scenographia Totius Fabricae S. LauRentii In Escoriali"

        v. 37 x 47cm   p. 41 x 52cm   Hand-colored
        Text on verso
        [Braun & Hogenberg, v. 6, no. 4]
        Location: SHSW

FAIRHAVEN, WA

"Fairhaven, Washington 1891."

        v. 59 x 99cm   p. 69 x 106cm   Black & white
        Sketch of B. W. Pierce.
        Litho. Elliot Pub Co. 120 Sutter St. S[an] F[rancisco]
        Presented by the Fairhaven Land Co.
        Location: SHSW

FAMAGUSTA, CYPRUS

"Famaugusta."

        v. 9 x 12cm   p. 41 x 55cm   Hand-colored
        Text on verso
        [Braun & Hogenberg, v. 1, no. 51]
        Location: SHSW

FLORENCE, ITALY

"Florentia"

>   v. 17 x 48cm   p. 41 x 55cm   Hand-colored
>   Text on verso
>   [Braun & Hogenberg, v. 1 no. 45]
>   Location: SHSW

FORT MADISON, IA

"Perspective Map of Fort Madison, IA. 1889."

>   v. 37 x 95cm   p. 50 x 101cm   Black & white
>   H. Wellge SK.
>   Copyrighted and Published by American Publishing Co.
>   205 Second St. Milwaukee, Wis.
>   Insets: Extension from Cor. Santa Fe and Union Ave.;
>   S. & J. C. Atlee; C. N. Ross; The Knapp Stout
>   & Co. Company; Peters & Bernhard Company;
>   The Fort Madison and Appanoose Stone Company;
>   Hotel Anthes; Morrison Manufacturing Co's Plow Works;
>   Mills of the Fort Madison Paper Co.; New Bank
>   Building
>   Location: SHSW
>   Library of Congress

FRANKFURT, WEST GERMANY

"Civitas Francofordiana Ad Moe"

>   v. 34 x 48cm   p. 41 x 56cm   Hand-colored
>   Text on verso
>   [Braun & Hogenberg, v. 1, no. 36]
>   Location: SHSW

GENOA, ITALY

"Genua."

>   v. 17 x 48cm   p. 41 x 55cm   Hand-colored
>   Text on verso
>   [Braun & Hogenberg, v. 1, no. 45]
>   Location: SHSW

GRANADA, SPAIN

"Granata"

>   v. 38 x 49cm   p. 42 x 53cm   Hand-colored
>   Text on verso
>   Effigiabat Georgius Houfnaglius Anno MDLXV
>   [Braun & Hogenberg, v. 5, no. 13]
>   Location: SHSW

HAMBURG, WEST GERMANY

"Hamburgum"

>   v. 38 x 48cm   p. 42 x 53cm   Hand-colored
>   Text on verso
>   [Braun & Hogenberg, v. 4, no. 36]
>   Location: SHSW

HURON, SD

"Huron, Beadle County, Dakota." 1883

>   v. 26 x 46cm   p. 34 x 51cm   Black & white
>   Wm. Valentine Herancourt. Delr. January 1883.
>   Printed at the Office of the Daily Times Huron, Dakota
>   Insets: Machine Shops and Roundhouse of the C & N.W.
>   Ry. Co.; Huron Public School
>   Location: SHSW

ISPEMING, MI

"Bird's Eye View of Ishpeming. L. S. Michigan. 1871."

>   v. 38 x 51cm   p. 49 x 62cm   Tinted
>   Drawn by H. H. Bailey.
>   C. H. Vogt. Lith.
>   Print. Milwaukee Lith. & Engr. Co.
>   Location: SHSW
>   Marquette County [MI] Historical Society

LISBON, PORTUGAL

"Olissipo quae nunc Lisboa, civitas amplissima Lusitaniae,
ad Tagum."

        v. 37 x 47cm   p. 42 x 53cm   Hand-colored
        Text on verso
        [Braun & Hogenberg, v. 5, no. 2]
        Location: SHSW

LIVERMORE, CA

[Bird's-Eye View of Livermore in 1889]

        v. n.a.   p. n.a.   n.a.
        Pub by W. W. Elliott
        Lith. Schmidt Label & Lith. Co.
        Facsimile, 1974, by Livermore Herald
        Location: SHSW - copy

MALTA

"Malta."

        v. 9 x 12cm   p. 41 x 55cm   Hand-colored
        Text on verso
        [Braun & Hogenberg, v. 1, no. 51]
        Location: SHSW

MANTUA, ITALY

"Mantua"

        v. 36 x 50cm   p. 41 x 54cm   Hand-colored
        Text on verso
        [Braun & Hogenberg, v. 2, no. 50]
        Location: SHSW

MARIENBERG, EAST GERMANY

"Marienberg Misniae Civitas"

        v. 33 x 45cm   p. 42 x 53cm   Hand-colored
        Text on verso
        Depictuma Iacobo Haufnagel.
        [Braun & Hogenberg, v. 6, no. 19]
        Location: SHSW

MARSEILLE, FRANCE

"Marseille."

        v. 32 x 35cm   p. 41 x 55cm   Hand-colored
        Text on verso
        [Braun & Hogenberg, v. 2, no. 12]
        Location: SHSW

MESSINA, SICILY

"Messana,"

        v. 34 x 49cm   p. 41 x 57cm   Hand-colored
        Text on verso
        [Braun & Hogenberg, v. 1, no. 50]
        Location: SHSW

MOSCOW, U.S.S.R.

"Moscovia urbs Metropolis Totius Russiae Albae."

        v. 35 x 46cm   p. 42 x 52cm   Hand-colored
        Text on verso
        [Braun & Hogenberg, v. 6 no. 54]
        Location: SHSW

NAPLES, ITALY

"Haec est nobilis, a florens illa Neapolis,"

        v. 34 x 48cm   p. 41 x 56cm   Hand-colored
        Text on verso
        [Braun & Hogenberg, v. 1, no. 48]
        Location: SHSW

"Elegantissimus ad mare Tyrrhenum ex monte Pausilipo Neapolis
montifque Vesnuij prospechus."

        v. 37 x 49cm   p. 41 x 53cm   Hand-colored
        Text on verso
        Depinxit Georgius Houfnaglius Anno 1578.
        [Braun & Hogenberg, v. 5, no. 65]
        Location: SHSW

NEW YORK CITY, NY

"Panoramic View of New York City and Vicinity." 1912

        v. 51 x 71cm   p. 56 x 74cm   Tinted
        United States Printing & Lithograph Co, New York
        Copyright 1912 by Jacob Ruppert.
        Location: SHSW

NIAGARA FALLS, NY

"Niagara's Great Gorge Trip   The Falls and Whirlpool Rapids
Route" 1930

        v. 20 x 79cm   p. 22 x 81cm   Tinted
        C. F. Adams
        The Whitney-Graham Co. Buffalo & New York, c1930
        Location: SHSW

NICARAGUA

"Bird's-Eye View of the Interoceanic Canal of Nicaragua and
Costa Rica" [n.d.]

>   v. 49 x 84cm   p. 63 x 97cm   Tinted
>   Compiled from official data by Fred K Leuthner
>   Lithographed by Julius Bien & Co. N[ew] Y[ork]
>   Location: SHSW

"Bird's-Eye View of the Maritime Canal of Nicaragua." [1890?]

>   v. 50 x 84cm   p. 62 x 97cm   Tinted
>   American Bank-Note Co.-New York-U.S.A.
>   [Variant copy of preceding entry]
>   Location: SHSW

OAKLAND, CA

"Bird's Eye View of Oakland & Vicinity Alameda Co. California."
[1887]

>   v. 51 x 76cm   p. 59 x 82cm   Black & white
>   Lith. Britton & Rey S[an] F[rancisco]
>   Specially prepared and presented by the Oakland Tribune
>   Location: SHSW

OSTEND, BELGIUM

"Ostenda"

>   v. 35 x 46cm   p. 42 x 53cm   Hand-colored
>   Text on verso
>   [Braun & Hogenberg, v. 6, no. 11]
>   Location: SHSW

PALERMO, SICILY

"Palermo."

>   v. 33 x 50cm   p. 42 x 53cm   Hand-colored
>   Text on verso
>   [Braun & Hogenberg, v. 4, no. 56]
>   Location: SHSW

PANAMA CANAL

"Bird's-Eye View of the Panama Canal" 1912

        v. 21 x 45cm   p. 25 x 48cm   Tinted
        H. H. Green
        Supplement to the National Geographic Magazine
            (Washington, D.C.), February, 1912, Gilbert
        Location: SHSW

PAPA, HUNGARY

"Papa, Inferioris Hungariae Oppidum."

        v. 33 x 49cm   p. 41 x 53cm   Hand-colored
        Text on verso
        Communicavit G. Houfnaglius.
        Acceptum a Philippo Fernandeo:
        [Braun & Hogenberg, v. 6, no. 35]
        Location: SHSW

PLATTSBURGH, NY

"Plattsburgh 1899"

        v. 46 x 81cm   p. 58 x 91cm   Black & white
        C. Fausel, Artist
        L. R. Burleigh Lith. N[ew] Y[ork]
        Location: SHSW
                Library of Congress

PRAGUE, CZECHOSLOVAKIA

"Palatium Imperatorum Pragae Quod vulgo Ratzin Appellatur"

"Praga Regni Bohemiae metropolis"

        v. 37 x 49cm   p. 42 x 53cm   Hand-colored
        Text on verso
        [Braun & Hogenberg, v. 5, no. 49]
        Location: SHSW

RAPID CITY, SD

"Rapid City, Pennington County Dakota" 1883

       v. 29 x 50cm   p. 31 x 56cm   Black & white
       W. V. Herancourt, del Oct 1st. '83
       Insets: Pennington Co. Court House; Rapid City
              Public School
       Location: SHSW

REGENSBURG, WEST GERMANY

"Ratis Bona"

       v. 35 x 49cm   p. 42 x 53cm   Hand-colored
       Text on verso
       Effigiavit Jacobus Houfnaglius Geor:fil in Comitijs
         Ratisbonensibus Anno 1594
       [Braun & Hogenberg, v. 5, no. 51]
       Location: SHSW

RHODES

"Rhodus"

       v. 9 x 12cm   p. 41 x 55cm   Hand-colored
       Text on verso
       [Braun & Hogenberg, v. 1, no. 51]
       Location: SHSW

RIDGEWAY, PA

"Ridgeway, Elk County Pennsylvania. 1895."

       v. n.a.   p. n.a.   n.a.
       Drawn by T.M. Fowler, Morrisville PA
       Published by T.M. Fowler & James B. Moyer
       Copyright by T.M. Fowler & James B. Moyer
       Facsimile, 1974, by Ridgeway Sesquicentennial Committee
       Location: SHSW
              Library of Congress

ROME, ITALY

"Roma."

        v. 34 x 49cm   p. 41 x 56cm   Hand-colored
        Text on verso
        [Brown & Hogenberg, v. 1, no. 46]
        Location: SHSW

"Antiquae urbis Romae Imago Accuratiss."

        v. 68 x 50cm   p. 76 x 53cm   Hand-colored
        Text on verso
        [Braun & Hogenberg, v. 4, no. 54 & 55]
        Location: SHSW

ROTTERDAM, NETHERLANDS

"Roterodamum,"

        v. 30 x 39cm   p. 42 x 52cm   Hand-colored
        Text on verso
        [Braun & Hogenberg, v. 4, no. 13]
        Location: SHSW

ROSTOCK, EAST GERMANY

"Rostochium Urbs Vandalica Anseatica Et Megapolitana"

        v. 36 x 49cm   p. 42 x 53cm   Hand-colored
        Text on verso
        [Braun & Hogenberg, v. 5, no. 47]
        Location: SHSW

ST. PAUL, AUSTRIA

"S. Polid vulgo San Polten"

        v. 30 x 47cm   p. 41 x 53cm   Hand-colored
        Communicavit Georgius Houfnaglius delinatum afilio
           Iacobo ao. 1617
        [Braun & Hogenberg, v. 6, no. 24]
        Location: SHSW

                         SAN DIEGO, CA

"San Diego, Cal." [1887]

          v. 37 x 64cm   p. 54 x 72cm   Black & white
          W. W. Elliott Pub. S[an] F[rancisco]
          Published by the San Diego Union Company.
          Location: SHSW

"Birdseye View of San Diego City and Harbor, showing Panama-
California Exposition Site." [1914]

          v. 19 x 55cm   p. 22 x 56cm   Black & white
          Schwartz & Ewing Studio
          Inset: U. S. Grant Hotel
          Location: SHSW

                         SANDUSKY, OH

"View of the City of Sandusky, O." [n.d.]

          v. 54 x 112cm   p. 69 x 124cm   Tinted
          Drawn on Stone & Printed in Oil Colors by Middleton,
              Wallace & Co. Lithos. 115 Walnut St. Cincinnati, O.
          Published by J. T. Palmatary
          Location: SHSW

                       SAN FRANCISCO, CA

"San Francisco The Exposition City" 1912

          v. 71 x 108cm   p. 81 x 112cm   Tinted
          Pingree-Traung Co. Lith. S.F.
          Copyright by North American Press Ass'n
              1912 Hearst Bldg. S[an] F[rancisco]
          Location: SHSW

SAN PEDRO, CA

"San Pedro, Los Angeles Co., California." [n.d.]

> v. 55 x 80cm   p. 56 x 82cm   Black & white
> Drawn & Litho'd by B. W. Pierce, 230, N. Main St.
>   L.A. Cal.
> Inset: Buildings of F. Wiedwald; Harbor View Hotel;
>   Residence of R.D. Sepulveda; Residence of J.H.
>   Dodson; Public School Building; Bank of San
>   Pedro; Residence of Geo. H. Peck; Residence of Ed-
>   quard Amar; Eisen's General Merchandise Store;
>   Clay Building; Episcopal Church; Palace Bath
>   House; Property of [   ].R. Poggi; G. Falk;
>   M E Church; Public Library; Catholic Church;
>   Property of Julius Seick; Presbyterian Church
> Location: SHSW

STOCKHOLM, SWEDEN

"Stocholm"

> v. 33 x 47cm   p. 42 x 53cm   Hand-colored
> Text on verso
> Two views of the City from different directions.
> Donabathuic operi, Hieronymus Scholeus.
> [Braun & Hogenberg, v. 4, no. 38]
> Location: SHSW

STOCKTON, CA

"Stockton Looking East. San Joaquin County, Cal." [n.d.]

> v. 53 x 90cm   p. 61 x 97cm   Black & white
> Sketched by C. P. Cook
> W. W. Elliot Lith. S[an] F[rancisco]
> Insets: St. Agnes Academy; Jefferson School; Stockton
>   Combined Harvester & Agricultural Works; view
>   of a garden; San Joaquin County Court House;
>   Stockton Pharmacy; Avon Block; A Public School;
>   Hardware Store; Yosemite House; U. S. Hotel;
>   Office of the Stockton Daily & Weekly Independent

                    Austin Bros; Stockton Business College;
                    Stockton Insane Asylum; H. C. Shaw Corps;
                    The Pacific Asylum; The Matteson & Williamson
                    Mfg. Co.; scene in Stockton Harbor; Masonic
                    Temple; Stockton Wheel Co. Enterprise Planing Mill;
                    Agricultural Pavilion; Stockton Planing Mill;
                    Grand Central Hotel; Commercial Hotel
          Location: SHSW

SULMONA, ITALY

"Sulmo Ovidii Patria."

          v. 33 x 26cm   p. 42 x 53cm   Hand-colored
          Text on verso
          [Braun & Hogenberg, v. 4. no. 52]
          Location: SHSW

TACOMA, WA

"Picture-Map of Camp Lewis American Lake (Tacoma) Washington"
1918

          v. 22 x 58cm   p. 24 x 62cm   Tinted
          Text & maps of area on verso
          Cover title: Birdeye view of Camp Lewis
          Copyrighted 1918 by Seattle Engraving Co.
          Location: SHSW

TILLSONBURG, ONTARIO

"Tilsonburg, Ontario. 1881."

          v. 30 x 49cm   p. 35 x 51cm   n.a.
          T. M. Fowler, SE.
          Beck & Pauli, Lith. Milwaukee, Wis.
          Pub. by Fowler & Rhines
          Insets: Tillson Block; Sinclair Block; E.D.
                   Tillson's Mills
          Facsimile by Tillsonburg & District Historical Museum
               Society reprint. 1975
          Location: SHSW

TOLEDO, SPAIN

"Toletum."

        v. 38 x 51cm   p. 42 x 53cm   Hand-colored
        Text on verso
        Depingebat Georgius Houfnaglius Ao. 1566
        [Braun & Hogenberg, v. 5, no. 15]
        Insets: Palatium Regium Toletanum; Templum
                Archiepiscopat, Toletani
        Location: SHSW

TOURS, FRANCE

"Turones vulgo Tours le Jardin de France."

        v. 18 x 24cm   p. 42 x 52cm   Hand-colored
        Text on verso
        Delineavit G. Houfnaglius Anno Dni 1561
        [Braun & Hogenberg, v. 5, no. 20]
        Location: SHSW

TUSKEGEE, AL

"Buildings and Grounds of Tuskegee Normal and Industrial
Institute, Tuskegee, Alabama." [n.d.]

        v. n.a.   p. n.a.   n.a.
        Franklin Co. Eng-Chi[cago]
        Location: SHSW

URBINO, ITALY

"Urbino."

        v. 33 x 21cm   p. 42 x 53cm   Hand-colored
        Text on verso
        Two views of Urbino from different directions
        [Braun & Hogenberg, v. 4, no. 52]
        Location: SHSW

VENICE, ITALY

"Venetia."

> v. 34 x 48 cm   p. 41 x 56cm   Hand-colored
> Text on verso
> [Braun & Hogenberg, v. 1, no. 44]
> Inset: [city officials in contemporary clothing]
> Location: SHSW

VERONA, ITALY

"Verona"

> v. 36 x 47cm   p. 41 x 55cm   Hand-colored
> Text on verso
> Two different views of city.
> [Braun & Hogenberg, v. 3, no. 49]
> Location: SHSW

VIENNA, AUSTRIA

"Vienna Austriae"

> v. 32 x 49cm   p. 42 x 53cm   Hand-colored
> Text on verso
> [Braun & Hogenberg, v. 6, no. 21]
> Location: SHSW

WASHINGTON D.C.

"Birdseye View of the National Capital Including the Site of th
Proposed World's Exposition of 1892 and Permanent Exposition of
the Three Americas." 1888

> v. 60 x 90cm   p. 68 x 93cm   Tinted
> Lith. by A. Hoen & Co. Baltimore
> Copyright, 1888 by E. Kurtz Johnson, Treasurer
>   Board of Promotion.
> Location: SHSW

ADDENDUM

BERLIN

"Berlin, Wis. 1892."

        v. 35 x 56cm   p. 46 x 61cm   n.a.
        C. J. Pauli
        Drawn & Published by C. J. Pauli, Milwaukee, Wis.
        Location: SHSW-copy
              Berlin Historical Society, Berlin

NEW HOLSTEIN

[1879. Held by New Holstein Historical Society. Bibliographical
details as yet unavailable]

STEVENS POINT

"Bird's Eye View of the City of Stevens Point. Portage Co.
Wis. 1874."

        v. n.a.   p. n.a.   n.a.
        Drawn & Published by A. J. Cleveland
        American Oleograph Co. Milwaukee, Wis.
        Location: SHSW-copy

CHICAGO, IL

[Downtown Chicago] 1898

        v. 94 x 145cm   p. 101 x 153cm   Tinted
        Copyright, 1898 by Poole Bros. Chicago, Ill.
        Location: SHSW
              Library of Congress

GETTYSBURG, PA

"Gettysburg Battle-field." 1863

      v. 53 x 92cm   p. 71 x 101cm   Tinted
      Jno. B. Bachelder, Del.
      Endicott & Co. Lith. N.Y.
      Entered according to Act of Congress in the Year 1863
         by Jno. B. Bachelder in the Clerks Office of the
         District of Massachusetts.
      Inset: plan of the Soldiers National Cemetery.
      Location: SHSW

"Perspective View of Gettysburg National Military Park" 1916

      v. 43 x 54cm   p. 48 x 60cm   Tinted
      Drawing Made February, 1916, by Lieut.-Colonel
         E.B. Cope, Engineer
      Location: SHSW